THE ABCDEFG

OF

SALVATION

Peter Currie

© September 2018 Peter Currie
First published 2018
Second edition 2022

A catalogue for this book is available from the British Library
ISBN 978-1-84625-628-8

Distributed by Day One Publications
Ryelands Road, Leominster HR6 8NZ

Tel 01568 613 740
Fax 01568 611 473
email: sales@dayone.co.uk
website: www.dayone.co.uk

Printed by Helloprint, 100 Pall Mall, St James, London SW1Y 5NQ
Tel. 020 3695 4056   www.helloprint.co.uk

Introduction

Some of my readers will have heard of the ABC of becoming a Christian. However, some time ago, I thought of trying to extend this to include the Christian life and the certain hope of heaven. This little booklet is the result.

I did not write it with theologians in mind, but for ordinary people who appreciate simple things, plainly put. However, for the avoidance of doubt, I would like to affirm that I believe that the great sacrifice of Calvary is sufficient for all mankind, though we only derive benefit from it when we put our trust in the Lord Jesus Christ. I would also like to affirm the necessity of repentance – we should repent and we need to, but the wonderful thing to me is that, when sinners genuinely trust in the Saviour, they do repent. I hope and pray that this will be the experience of all who read this little booklet.

Unless otherwise indicated, Bible quotations are from the New King James Version.

Peter Currie
London
September 2018

ALL HAVE
SINNED

A stands for 'All have sinned'

The subject of this booklet is 'The ABCDEFG of Salvation'. Let us start with 'A'. The Bible says 'All have sinned and fall short of the glory of God' (Romans 3:23). A stands for 'All have sinned'. But what is sin? Sin is breaking God's law, the Ten Commandments.

I wonder. Do you remember what they are? You will find them in Exodus chapter twenty. In the first commandment, God says 'I am the LORD your God ... You shall have no other gods'. Nothing and no one must be allowed to take God's rightful place in our lives. The second commandment says 'You shall not bow down to [idols]' and yet all over the world there are people who do that. The third commandment says 'You shall not take the name of the LORD your God in vain'. The way we speak the name of God and the Lord Jesus Christ, whether reverently or the opposite, shows what He means to us, and, if we take His name in vain, He specifically says that He will not hold us guiltless. The fourth commandment is the one that tells us to keep Sunday special. It is the day of rest and the day when we have time to think about God.

The fifth commandment says that we should be respectful to our parents and then there are those five commandments telling us not to murder, not to commit adultery, not to steal, not to bear false witness and not to covet. What a happy place this world would be, if only people obeyed the Ten Commandments!

We should obey them because God says we should. He is our Creator and He has the right to tell us what we should do, but the bad news is that we have all broken God's Ten Commandments and we deserve to be punished. There is a fearful prospect beyond death for those who are not trusting in the Lord Jesus Christ as their Saviour, but the good news is that 'Christ Jesus came into the world to save sinners' (1 Timothy 1:15).

BEHOLD!
THE LAMB

B stands for 'Behold! The Lamb'

A stands for 'All have sinned', but B stands for 'Behold! The Lamb'. When John the Baptist saw Jesus coming towards him, he said 'Behold! The Lamb of God who takes away the sin of the world!' (John 1:29). He was thinking of the Passover lamb that was sacrificed in Old Testament times. God taught His people that if their sins were going to be forgiven, a substitute had to die; blood had to be shed.

Of course, the blood of a lamb or a goat or a bull could not really take away sin. This is why the Lord Jesus had to die. He was the true Lamb of God who took away sin by the shedding of His precious blood when He died upon the Cross of Calvary. Our sin and guilt were 'laid on Him' in such a way that He was treated as though He were the sinner and was punished instead, 'the Just for the unjust' (see Isaiah 53:6; 1 Peter 3:18).

The great sacrifice of Calvary is of infinite worth because of the wonderful Person who died there – the sinless Son of God, equal with God the Father, who became Man and went to the Cross for us people and for our salvation, and rose again in victory on the third day.

> He died that we might be forgiven,
> He died to make us good,
> That we might go at last to heaven,
> Saved by His precious blood.
>
> There was no other good enough
> To pay the price of sin;
> He only could unlock the gate
> Of heaven, and let us in.

COME
TO ME

C stands for 'Come to Me'

It is most wonderful that the Son of God should come down from heaven to save us, but we need to respond, we need to turn from sin and turn to Him, and this is why C stands for 'Come to Me'.

That is what Jesus said. He said 'Come to Me, all you who ... [are weary and] heavy laden, and I will give you rest' (Matthew 11:28). Do you remember John Bunyan's immortal allegory, The Pilgrim's Progress? It begins by saying that he 'dreamed a dream' in which he saw 'a man clothed with rags, standing in a certain place, with his face from his own house, a book in his hand, and a great burden upon his back'. The great burden represents our sins which are like a heavy burden which is too heavy for us to bear. I wonder. Do your sins feel like that? Do you feel the heavy burden of your sins and do you want something done about it?

When people feel this heavy burden, the Lord Jesus steps in and says 'come to Me ... and I will give you rest'. This means the rest of conscience that comes from knowing that 'the blood of Jesus Christ [God's] Son cleanses us from all sin' (1 John 1:7). When Bunyan's Christian came to the Cross, 'his burden loosed from off his shoulders, and fell from off his back, and began to tumble, and so continued to do, till it came to the mouth of the sepulchre, where it fell in, and I saw it no more'. The great burden which had troubled Christian in the City of Destruction and weighed him down in the Slough of Despond, now fell from off his back of its own accord. Burdens are lifted at Calvary and nowhere else.

If you have never done so, I urge you to come to the Lord Jesus Christ and put your trust in Him as your Saviour, in Him alone. He says 'come to Me ... and I will give you rest'. Amen!

Thursday 12 FEB
FRIDAY 13 FeB
SAturday 14 FeB

DISCIPLES

Sunday 15 FEB: Dep. to Sutton.

Important to discuss ~~FEB~~
my details with Diana on
Saturday 14 FeB

From 12 FEB 2023

D stands for 'Disciples'

If you genuinely come to the Lord Jesus Christ and put your trust in Him as your Saviour, that makes you a Christian. It is the end of being weighed down by the burden of sin, but it is also the start of an adventure, just as it was for Christian in The Pilgrim's Progress. It is the start of being a real disciple of the Lord Jesus. In the Great Commission, the Lord told His apostles to 'Go therefore and make *disciples* of all the nations' (Matthew 28:19a). D stands for 'Disciples'.

The New Testament was originally written in Greek and the Greek word for disciple literally means a learner. To start with, we learn the ABC of becoming a Christian through the proclamation of the gospel, but the Lord Jesus also told His apostles to give further teaching to those who become Christians – 'teaching them to observe all things that I have commanded you' (Matthew 28:20a), He said.

If you genuinely come to the Lord Jesus Christ and put your trust in Him as your Saviour, you will be glad to acknowledge Him as the Lord of your life, as well. You will want to follow Him and obey His commands. You will want to be a real disciple of the Lord Jesus.

Perhaps, you have only recently become a Christian or, perhaps, although you have been a Christian for some time, you would like to get back to basics and go through some basic Christian teaching again. Well, a few years ago, I wrote a book published by Day One, entitled 'What happens when ... ?', which provides answers to questions for new Christians. I think you will find it helpful!

EVERY
CREATURE

E stands for 'Every creature'

So then, D stands for 'Disciples' and E stands for 'Every creature'. The Lord Jesus told His apostles to 'Go into all the world and preach the gospel to every creature' (Mark 16:15). When we have trusted in the Lord Jesus Christ and are sure of our salvation, it is only natural that we should want to tell others about what means so much to us. It reminds me of that old chorus:

> *Everybody should know,*
> *Everybody should know,*
> *I have such a wonderful Saviour*
> *That everybody should know.*

Yes, we are to 'Go into all the world and preach the gospel to [everybody]'. This is the great task of the Christian church and if we are real Christians, then we should seek to play our part.

We cannot all be up front speakers, but we should be 'ready always to give an answer' when people ask us questions about our faith (1 Peter 3:15, KJV), and there are times when we should be proactive in seeking to win others.

This was the case with Andrew, Simon Peter's brother. When Andrew heard about the Lord Jesus Christ and started to follow Him, he was so enthusiastic that he did not wait for Peter to ask questions. Instead, he went and found his brother and told him, 'We have found the Messiah!' and the Bible says 'he brought him to Jesus' (see John 1:41-42).

We can do the same. It may not be a brother or sister, but surely there is someone we can pray for and speak to and seek to bring to Jesus.

FELLOWSHIP

F stands for 'Fellowship'

Simon Peter genuinely loved the Lord Jesus Christ, but in a moment of weakness, he denied his Lord three times with oaths and curses. You probably know the story – it is recorded in all four Gospels. However, let us go forward in time just over seven weeks. It is the day of Pentecost. The place is Jerusalem and a large crowd has gathered. A man raises his voice and begins to address the crowd. Who is he? The same man who was such a coward just a short time before. What a change has taken place!

Simon Peter had been forgiven by the Lord Jesus and he had also been given the power to be different. Peter spoke boldly to the people about the Resurrection. He told them 'It's really true! We have seen the risen Lord'. Peter also spoke boldly to the people about their great sin of rejecting the Lord Jesus Christ (Acts 2:32 and 36).

Now when they heard this, the Bible says the people were 'cut to the heart' (Acts 2:37a). They realised they had done something very wrong. I wonder if you have ever felt like that? You know you have done something very wrong and you wish you had not done it. Well, these people were the same and they said to Peter and the other apostles, 'Men and brethren, what shall we do?' (Acts 2:37b).

In reply, Peter urged them to 'repent', that is, to change their attitude to the Lord Jesus Christ and 'be saved' (Acts 2:38a and 40). Many of the people responded to what Peter said to them and about three thousand were baptized as a public confession of their faith in the Lord Jesus Christ. How happy they were as a result. Their sins were forgiven and there was a new power at work in their lives. The Bible says 'they continued steadfastly in the apostles' ... [teaching] and fellowship' (Acts 2:42a).

This is my letter F – F stands for 'Fellowship'. Christians belong together. The Bible says that we should not forsake 'the assembling of ourselves together' (Hebrews 10:25a). When I was young, we used to have a real coal fire in our home. The coals glowed red – how hot they were! However, if a coal came out of the fire, it would not stay hot and glowing for long. Likewise, Christians, to prevent their love from growing cold, need to meet together for mutual encouragement. F stands for 'Fellowship'.

GLORY to DIANA

The anguish of my soul
to see you suffer... I have
heard the cry of distress.

G stands for 'Glory'

Yes, F stands for 'Fellowship' and, finally, G stands for 'Glory'. We started with Romans 3:23 which says that 'All have sinned and fall short of the glory of God', but I want to go on now to Romans 5:1-2 which says: 'Therefore, having been justified by faith, we have peace with God through our Lord Jesus Christ, through whom also we have access by faith into this grace in which we stand, and rejoice in hope of the glory of God'.

The Bible says there is a heaven to gain and a hell to shun. Because we are sinners, we do not have the right to enter the glory of heaven – we fall short of the glory of God. However, if we have trusted in the Lord Jesus Christ and are sure of our salvation, the Bible says we can 'rejoice in hope of the glory of God'. We can look forward to heaven.

Of course, the bitter must come before the sweet. The upward path that leads us home is not an easy road. The Bible says that 'we must through many tribulations enter the kingdom of God' (Acts 14:22b). However, it also says that our Saviour will never leave us nor forsake us (Hebrews 13:5b).

Yes, the Lord Jesus is the Lamb of God who takes away the sin of all who come to Him and put their trust in Him. He will give you rest from the burden of sin, He will lead you all the way through life and then He will welcome you to the wonderful home He has prepared for us in the Glory. Trust Him today!

> Come, then, and join this holy band,
> And on to glory go
> To dwell in that celestial land
> Where joys immortal flow.

> *Only trust Him, only trust Him,*
> *Only trust Him now;*
> *He will save you, He will save you,*
> *He will save you now.*

Amen!